How to be a Pop Star

by David Orme

Trailblazers

How to be a Pop Star
by David Orme
Educational consultant: Helen Bird

Illustrated by Martin Bolchover

Published by Ransom Publishing Ltd.
Rose Cottage, Howe Hill, Watlington, Oxon. OX49 5HB
www.ransom.co.uk

ISBN   184167 594 6

          978 184167 594 7

First published in 2006

Copyright © 2006 Ransom Publishing Ltd.

Illustrations copyright © 2006 Martin Bolchover

'Get the Facts' section - images copyright: rock band - Lise Gagne; goth musicians - Sharon Dominick; acoustic guitar -Julie Deshaies; website courtesy Off The Radar; electric guitar - Don Oehman; sequencer workstation - Jeremiah Thompson; guy screaming - Nick Schlax; Africa map - Peeter Viisimaa; rapper - Greg Nicholas; mixing desk - Mike Bentley; vinyl LP - Meredith Lamb; rock concert and singer - Damir Cudic; grunge city band - Jennifer Trenchard; rock guitarists - Robert Kohlhuber; girl with cap - Nick Free.

How to be a Pop Star

Contents

How to be a

pop
star

Get
the
facts

So you want to be a pop star?

Getting started

- Get some lessons and learn some music **skills**!

- Get a group of together. Don't ask people just because they are **mates**. If you want to be successful, you need **talent**. You could put an advert in the local paper for musicians.

- Decide what sort of music you want to play. You could copy your heroes! You can buy practice CDs with your instrument missed out.

- **Practice** – but don't forget your neighbours may not like your sort of music!

Remember: it's not enough just to sound good.

You have to look and act like a pop star!

Getting a gig

No one is going to pay to hear an unknown band.

Start by performing

 at school.

 at your local youth club.

 at family weddings or parties.

 at local 'showcase' events. (Talent scouts often come to these.)

Getting known

Make yourself known! You could

 Build your own website.

 Make a recording.

Instruments

All sorts of instruments have been used in bands. The most popular are **guitars**, **keyboards**, and **drums**.

Always buy the best instruments you can afford.

Guitars

A band can have up to three guitars.

Lead guitar for playing solos.

Rhythm guitar

Bass guitar (a bass guitar has 4 strings.)

The guitars and keyboard will need amplifiers to make the sound really loud, though some artists play 'unplugged'. (This is using a guitar that is not amplified – it is called an acoustic guitar.)

8

Keyboards

These are played like a piano. Keyboards have switches to make lots of different sounds.

Drum kit

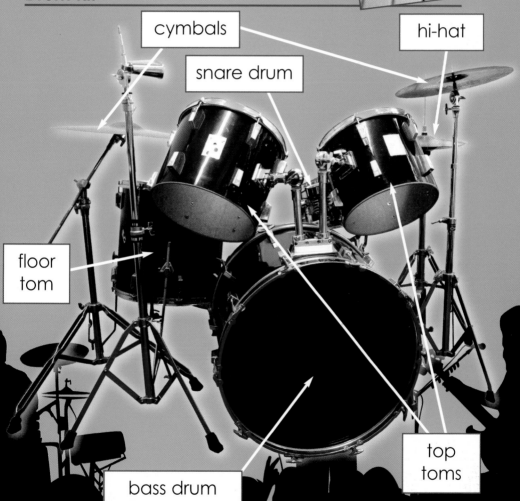

cymbals

hi-hat

snare drum

floor tom

top toms

bass drum

Timeline – history of pop

Type of music	What it was like	Famous bands & performers
1950s Rock and roll	Came from rhythm and blues and country music.	Bill Haley and the Comets, Elvis Presley
1960s Soul	Mix of rhythm and blues and gospel music.	Wilson Pickett, Otis Redding
1970s Reggae	Pop music from the Caribbean.	Bob Marley
Disco	Music for dancing. Used synthesisers.	ABBA
Punk rock	Loud, fast and nasty. Really annoyed most adults!	The Sex Pistols
New wave	Much gentler than punk. Adults approved!	Elvis Costello

Type of music	What it was like	Famous bands & performers
New romantics	Even gentler still – the boys wore make-up!	Duran Duran
Heavy metal	Very, VERY loud.	Iron Maiden, Black Sabbath
1980s Grunge	Mix of heavy metal and punk.	Nirvana
1990s – 2000s Hip hop	Music with spoken words - rap.	
Gangsta rap	Violent form of Hip hop. Words deal with city violence.	Eminem
Club music	Like disco, only for today's music fans. Electronic sounds and remixes per-formed by a DJ.	Fatboy Slim

Performing

Setting up

Get to the gig in good time.

Don't get in the way of people dealing with sound and lighting.

Make sure you have spare fuses, drum sticks and strings.

When you are set up, have a **sound check**. Get someone to stand in front of you and listen for the **balance** of the instruments.

Don't drink or take drugs. You might think you sound great, but no one else will.

The performance

Remember: **look good**, **sound good**.

Decide on an **image** and get the right clothes to match.

If possible make your own back drop. No one wants to look at a grotty wall.

Make sure you have enough songs.

In an evening you might perform two sets of songs of 45 minutes each.

Have a mix of slow and fast, loud and quiet songs. Don't forget to have a spare song for an **encore**!

Before you go on stage, warm up by playing chords or loosening up your voice.

13

Recording

How a recording studio works

What you need:

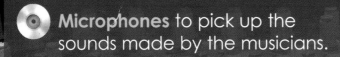

- **Microphones** to pick up the sounds made by the musicians.

- **Multitrack recorder**. This lets you record each artist separately.

  These used to use special recording tape. Now recordings are digital and are made on a hard disk.

- **Mixing console**. This lets the sound engineer mix the sounds together to make the best sound.

- **Reference loudspeakers**. These are god quality loudspeakers so the engineer can listen to the sounds from the players and from the mixing console.

The studio where the musicians play will be sound proofed. The room is specially made so that the music sounds as good as possible.

The famous Abbey Road studios in London.

Recording at home or at school

You don't need to go into a recording studio to record your band. You can do it at home - or at school.

Borrow or buy some cheap microphones and a tape recorder.

Experiment to get the best 'sound'. It's good practice too!

The Beatles - greatest band ever?

Beatles facts

Names:
John Lennon	rhythm guitar
Paul McCartney	bass guitar
George Harrison	lead guitar
Ringo Starr	drummer

Started out as: The Quarrymen in Liverpool, England.

Lennon, McCartney and Harrison played together for the first time in 1958.

Ringo Starr joined the band in 1962.

First hit: Love Me Do September 1962

First album: Please Please Me March 1963

Last concert in public: San Francisco, 29th August 1966

Break up of the band: 1970

The Beatles have sold over a billion records world wide!

They had over 50 hit singles, with 20 number ones in the USA.

They were the most successful pop band of the twentieth century.

Why were they important?

Their music was very original. Nobody played that kind of music before.

They wrote their own songs. That was a big change too.

People copied their music and the way they dressed.

Every record they made was different. The Beatles were always ahead of other bands.

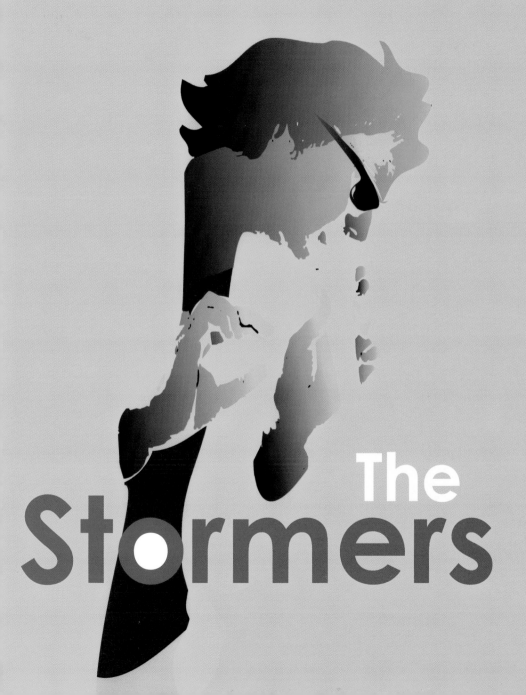

Chapter 1:
On their way

Phil Storm wrote great songs. He wanted to form a band with Nick and Terry.

But they couldn't afford to buy instruments.

Then something fantastic happened. When Phil got home he found a letter.

He had won five thousand pounds on his premium bonds!

His parents wanted him to save it.

"No way!" said Phil.

He rang the others.

"Music shop, Saturday morning. Fellers, we're on our way!"

Chapter 2:
Practice

At first, the Stormers were really, really bad. Then they were just – bad. Nick was pretty neat on keyboards, but Terry's drumming was crazy. Slowly he got it together.

Phil sang and played lead guitar.

His guitar playing was great.

His singing was terrible.

"The truth is, he's a rubbish performer," Nick said to Terry. "He writes great songs, but he can't put them over! Who's going to tell him?"

Phil's sister Simone told him. She listened to them practice – but not for long.

"Nick and Terry are O.K., and you are great on guitar, but you can't sing in tune. Face it, Phil, you're singing's AWFUL!"

But Phil wouldn't face it. What did kid sisters know anyway?

Nick and Terry knew Simone was right. If the band was going to make it, they had to dump Phil.

But Phil owned the instruments.

Chapter 3:
First gig

Phil had set up a gig at the youth club. Nick and Terry didn't think they were ready.

"We've got to go for it, gang," Phil said. "We'll be great, trust me."

Phil's singing hadn't got any better.

"He sounds like our cat locked out in the rain," Nick said.

Phil thought he sounded great.

They got to the club early. Simone came to help set up.

The youth leader gave them a great intro.

"Here's a new band that's going places! THE STORMERS!"

The first number started with instruments only. It sounded O.K., and people were enjoying it.

Then Phil started singing.

He was nervous, so it was even worse than usual.

It wasn't just bad.

It was really, REALLY bad.

Nick's cat would have done better.

The people in the club started to boo.

The youth leader went for a quiet lie down.

Phil glared at Nick and Terry. He thought people were booing them!

Chapter 4:
Keep playing!

The song ended. People had hands over their ears, but Phil ignored them. He played the first chords of the next number. He opened his mouth to sing.

Then he was barged away from the mike. Simone was on stage!

"Keep playing!" she hissed.

Simone started singing, and the crowd went quiet. She had a great voice! She knew Phil's songs well. A great cheer went up at the end, but Phil wasn't pleased.

"There's nothing wrong with my singing!"

After the gig, Terry and Nick tried to tell Phil the truth. But he didn't want to know. Simone came over. She took out her mobile phone. She had recorded the first song on it.

"Listen!"

Phil listened. Then he said "Turn it off!"

He looked round.

"Do I really sound as bad as that?"

Everyone nodded. "Yep!"

Phil looked at Simone.

"Sis, I hate you!"

"I hate you too!"

"So how about being our lead singer?"

"You're on!"

Simone had recorded Phil's singing.
Turn it off!
Am I really as bad as that?
Guess I'm the new lead singer!
My baaaybee lurves mee ...

How to be a pop star word check

acoustic	multitrack recorder
amplifier	musicians
artist	nervous
back drop	performer
balance	piano
chord	practice
encore	premium bonds
engineer	recording
famous	reference loudspeakers
gig	rhythm
guitar	skills
image	studio
instrument	successful
keyboard	talent
lead singer	talent scout
lighting	unknown
loosening	unplugged
microphones	website
mixing console	